MW01178178

12 SHORT HIKES

EAST BAY
SAN FRANCISCO
BAY AREA

NANCY SALCEDO

CHOCKSTONE PRESS
EVERGREEN, COLORADO

Cover photo by Clint Graves.

Book design by Jack Atkinson.

All uncredited photos within the book were taken by Nancy Salcedo.

ISBN: 1-57540-018-9

12 Short Hikes Series ISBN: 1-57540-022-7

Published and distributed by:
Chockstone Press, Inc.
Post Office Box 3505
Evergreen, Colorado 80437

This book is dedicated to Faith.

ACKNOWLEDGEMENTS

Thanks to Nick and Lu for hiking with me and Clint Graves for his photography. Thanks also to the staffs at the East Bay Regional Park District and Mount Diablo State Park, the staff at Chockstone Press, and Jim Ryder of Navajo Aviation for his insightful navigation.

INTRODUCTION

Short hikes in the East Bay stretch from the Suisun Marsh in the north to the Sunol Regional Wilderness in the south, and from the shores of San Francisco Bay in the west to Mount Diablo in the east. Just inland from the coast, the region is warmer and drier than much of the rest of the Bay Area, and gets quite hot in summer.

Much of the bay shore in the East Bay has been preserved or restored, with hiking access provided by the East Bay Regional Parks District. There is ample hiking in the hills above the bay, mostly through grasslands and oak groves. In leeward valleys, cool streams run through forested canyons. Farther east, the 3,849-foot peak of Mount Diablo rises above the valleys – the highest spot in the Bay Area and the ultimate vantage point.

Each hike, though varying in difficulty, terrain and views, has two key features in common. Each is less than two-and-a-half hours in duration, and each is within a hour's drive of Interstate 580, a main thoroughfare of the East Bay. Hikes are listed from south to north along Interstate 580, and from east to west in the hills.

COMPONENTS OF THIS GUIDE

Each hike is described on two facing pages. Following the hike and park names, you'll find a synopsis of trail length, duration, distance from the interstate and total elevation gain and loss. All statistics were obtained from trail maps, USGS topographic maps and on-site observations; their accuracy is not guaranteed.

Special characteristics of the hike are summarized in a brief passage that also includes directions on how to get to the trailhead. The elevation chart shows the ups and downs of the trail.

On the facing page, you'll find the trail shown on an aerial photograph of the area. Below the photo, the **Step by Step** guide briefly describes what you'll find along the path and how long it will take you to get from one point to another. This section is designed to help the hiker identify and stay on the route and to note interesting features along the trail. It's also a great way to coax along the more lackadaisical members of your hiking party.

The hiking times are approximate. I am a speedy hiker, but I brought my young son on each trail. The times do not include rest stops or picnic stops and are rounded to the nearest five-minute mark. Each hiker should set his or her own pace. Kids may slow you down a bit, but the trails are ideal for families.

HIKE WISELY

Generally, hiking in the Bay Area is a safe and fun way to pass the time. Though there are no guarantees, there is much you can do to ensure each outing is a safe and enjoyable one. What follows is an abbreviated list of hiking dos and don'ts, but it is by no means comprehensive. I encourage all hikers to verse themselves completely in the science of backcountry travel – it's knowledge worth having and it's easy to acquire. Written material on the subject is plentiful and easy to find at the nearest outdoors or sporting goods store.

FOR YOUR HEALTH

• Know the basics of first aid, including how to treat bleeding, bites and stings, and fractures, strains or sprains. Few of these hikes are so remote that help can't be reached within a short time, but you'd be wise to carry and know how to use simple supplies, such as over-the-counter pain relievers, bandages and ointments. Pack a first-aid kit on each excursion.

• Be prepared for the vagaries of Bay Area weather, as it changes quickly. The sun can cause you to overheat, so wear a hat and bring lots of water. Temperature changes are common – afternoon wind can pick up without warning and cooling fog can move in quickly, so bring extra clothes to layer on as needed.

FOR YOUR SAFETY

• Stay on the trail, well away from the edges of steep ravines and cliffs. Some (especially young) hikers enjoy climbing on rocks and cliffs, but many in the Bay Area are unstable, to the point that even venturing too near the edge could be extremely dangerous.

• If you are hiking with other people, stay with your group. Should one of the group become lost, he or she should sit down and stay put until found. Children should carry a whistle; if they become lost, they should blow it and/or shout loudly at regular intervals until found.

• The hills are home to an abundance of life, from gentle birds and fragrant wildflowers to rattlesnakes, stinging nettle, poison oak and poison hemlock. The Bay Area is a beautiful place, but can be unpredictable. To protect yourself and the environment, keep your hands to yourself. Don't pick the wildflowers – leave them for the next hiker to enjoy.

• Many trails venture briefly through pastures. Respect any livestock by keeping your distance, and they should do the same. Don't touch or feed any birds or

Contents

animals – they're best able to survive when self-reliant, and people-food is not what they need to thrive.

• There are ways to deal with the more dangerous critters in the wilds, like rattlesnakes and predators. Most will avoid you. Many parks post signs describing recent sitings and useful self-defense tactics should you encounter a potentially dangerous animal. Familiarize yourself with the proper etiquette.

FOR YOUR COMFORT

• Whether short and easy or long and strenuous, you'll enjoy each of these hikes much more if you wear good socks and hiking boots.

• Carry a comfortable backpack loaded with ample water or sport drink, snacks and/or a lunch and extra clothing, including a warm hat, gloves and a jacket.

• Maps are fun to have along, especially those that correspond to signposts along the trail.

• Bring whatever goodies interest you, like a camera, a field guide to help you identify wildflowers or birds, binoculars, a topographic map that identifies peaks and valleys, or a good novel to curl up with on a warm rock.

TRAIL USE

• Many of the trails described herein also are used by horseback riders and mountain bikers. Acquaint yourself with proper trail etiquette and be courteous.

• Many areas post gate and park hours in parking lots. Notice when the park closes and watch your time.

INDIAN JOE CREEK TRAIL TO CAVE ROCKS

Sunol Regional Wilderness

Trail Length:
2.3 miles

Drive Time From I-580 in Dublin:
20 minutes

Approx. Time:
1 hour, 30 min.

Elevation change:
600 feet

1 **Sunol Regional Wilderness** is in a remote valley just east of the city of Milpitas. Although cattle graze on this historic ranch land, there remain lots of signs of native wildlife. There is great bird-watching along Alameda Creek, with sitings of acorn woodpeckers and yellow-billed magpies common.

The hike is relatively strenuous as it climbs up through a rocky ravine, then through oaks and grassland to Cave Rocks. The return along Hayfield Road is easier, following a wide, gently descending trail through a pasture. The basalt outcrops at Cave Rocks may interest rock climbers. Park activities include hiking, picnicking and camping. No bikes or dogs are allowed. No fee.

To reach the trailhead from the intersection of Interstates 580 and 680 in Dublin, take I-680 south 7.5 miles to California Highway 84. Take Hwy. 84 south 4 miles to Geary Road. Head left (east) on Geary for 1.5 miles to the parking lot by the visitor center.

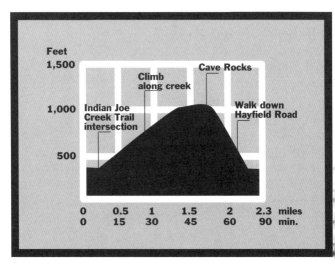

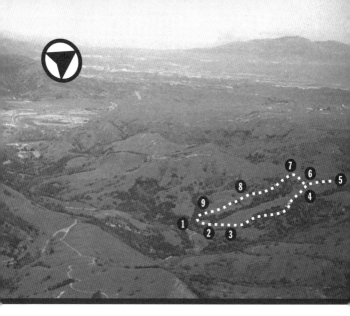

Step By Step

❶ Walk north from the parking area to the bridge just east of the visitor center. Cross the bridge and go right (east), on Indian Joe Nature Trail/Canyon View Trail.

❷ Pass intersections of Hayfield Road and Canyon View Trail, continuing straight (east) on Indian Joe Nature Trail to Indian Joe Creek Trail and turn left (north) up the hill (5 min.).

❸ Indian Joe Creek Trail climbs over a knoll, crosses a creek and turns left (north) through a cattle gate (15 min.).

❹ Continue up through a narrow canyon alongside Indian Joe Creek. The trail crosses the creek twice before reaching a ravine, then climbs away from the creek to the intersection of the cutoff trail to Hayfield Road to the right (50 min.).

❺ Continue straight (north) along Indian Joe Creek Trail to Cave Rocks (55 min.).

❻ Walk back to the intersection of the Hayfield Road cutoff (1 hour).

❼ Walk right (west) on the cutoff trail (check edit), traversing a steep ravine to Hayfield Road (1 hour, 10 min.).

❽ Walk left (south) down Hayfield Road through a pasture to the intersection of Indian Joe Nature Trail/Canyon View Trail (1 hour, 25 min.).

❾ Follow the signs right (west) to park headquarters and parking (1 hour, 30 min.).

"There is great bird-watching along Alameda Creek..."

BAY VIEW/MUSKRAT/ BOARDWALK LOOP

Coyote Hills Regional Park

Trail Length:
3.5 miles

Drive Time From
I-580 in San Leandro:
20 minutes

Approx. Time:
1 hour, 30 min.

Elevation change:
minimal

2

The Coyote Hills are grassy knolls over-looking the San Francisco Bay National Wildlife Refuge. Just east of the hills is a fresh-water marsh that hosts migratory birds and ducks. The hills stand out majestically in an otherwise flat area along the bay. Before dikes were built at the turn of the century, the bay's tides reached farther inland, making islands of the hills at high water.

The hike is easy, along a flat, paved (wheelchair-accessible) trail. Park activities include hiking, biking, horseback riding, picnicking and camping. There is a visitor center. No dogs, horses or bikes are allowed on the boardwalks in the marsh. There is a small fee.

To reach the trailhead from the intersection of Interstates 580 and 238 in San Leandro, take I-238 west 2 miles to I-880. Head south 10.3 miles on I-880 to CA Hwy. 84. Go west on Hwy. 84 for 1 mile to Decoto exit. Head right on Ardenwood Blvd. 1 mile to Commerce Drive. Head left 0.5 mile on Commerce to Patterson Ranch Road. Turn left (west) and follow Patterson Ranch to Coyote Hills Regional Park (fee area). Continue one mile to a parking area in front of the visitor center.

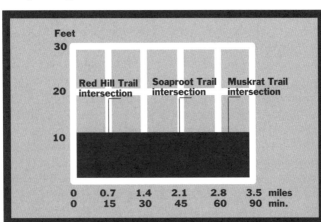

Step By Step

1 Walk west from the parking area through the gate. Go straight (west) along the paved Bay View Trail. (Refrain from the dirt road on the left.)

2 Continue northwest, between the marsh and the hills, past the intersection with the Nike Trail (5 min.).

3 Pass the intersection of the Red Hill Trail (15 min.).

4 Follow Bay View south, leaving the marsh, to the bench at the second intersection with the Nike Trail (30 min.).

5 Pass the intersection of Soaproot Trail (45 min.).

6 Bay View winds inland (east), past the intersection of No Name Trail (55 min.).

7 Continue around the hills on Bay View to the intersection of the Meadowlark Trail (1 hour).

8 Turn left (northeast), on Bay View and pass the Dairy Glen picnic area and the Quarry parking area (1 hour, 10 min.).

9 Cross Patterson Ranch Road to the intersection of Muskrat Trail (1 hour, 15 min.).

10 Go right, then immediately left on Muskrat, which takes you through the cattails. Walk atop a dike to signpost 5 on the left (west), which marks a viewing platform (1 hour, 20 min.).

11 Continue on Muskrat to the intersection of the trail back to the visitor center (1 hour, 25 min.).

12 Walk left (west) to a fork, again veering left on the boardwalk to cross Patterson Ranch Rd. and reach the parking area (1 hour, 30 min.).

HIGH RIDGE TRAIL/ VISTA PEAK TRAIL

Garin Regional Park

Trail Length:
3.4 miles

Drive Time From I-580 in San Leandro:
20 minutes

Approx. Time:
1 hr. 40 min.

Elevation change:
650 feet

3

Garin Regional Park is a historic ranch, and the old Garin Barn near the trailhead offers interpretive exhibits of its history. The hills surrounding the trail roll between cow pastures and wooded streambeds, with excellent views from the peaks.

The walk is relatively strenuous, along a good trail that is wide enough to be easily shared with bikes and horses. The route climbs along a creekbed, up into rolling hills of open grassland, then behind the hills down to the woods along the creek. Park activities include horseback riding, biking and hiking. No fee.

To reach the trailhead from the intersection of Interstates 580 and 238 in San Leandro, take I-238 (Foothill Blvd.) east 2 miles to I-238 (Mission Blvd.). Veer left and continue east on Mission Blvd. for 3.5 miles to Garin Avenue. Turn left on Garin Avenue and follow it to its end at the parking area of Garin Regional Park. Park in the north end of lot by the gate leading to High Ridge Trail.

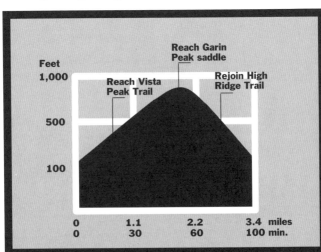

Step By Step

❶ Walk north, through the gate, along High Ridge Trail. The trail follows the creekbed to another gate at Arroyo Flats picnic area (5 min.).

❷ Leave the paved road as it turns to the left, and go straight (northeast), passing through a gate into open grassland. Follow High Ridge Trail, now a dirt road, to the intersection of the trail to Newt Pond (10 min.).

❸ Turn left (northwest) along High Ridge to the intersection of Vista Peak Trail (20 min.).

❹ Turn left and continue west along High Ridge through cow pastures and around the lower reaches of Garin and Vista Peaks to the second intersection with Vista Peak Trail (40 min.).

❺ Turn right (northeast) and follow Vista Peak Trail east around the backside of a rock outcropping atop Vista Peak. Continue to climb as the trail ascends a saddle near the exposed top of grass-covered Garin Peak (55 min).

❻ From this high point, the trail dives into the canyon behind Garin Peak, and winds down around hillsides to intersection of Zeile Creek Trail (1 hour).

❼ Stay on the Vista Peak Trail as it circles back to the west to rejoin the High Ridge Trail (1 hour, 20 min.).

❽ Turn down to the left (south) on High Ridge Trail and retrace your steps to the parking area (1 hour, 40 min.).

"The hills surrounding the trail (offer) excellent views..."

Marsh Trail to Cogswell Marsh

Hayward Regional Shoreline

Trail Length:
3.5 miles

Drive Time From
I-580 in San Leandro:
15 minutes

Approx. Time:
1 hour 50 min.

Elevation change:
minimal

4

The Hayward Regional Shoreline is home to many species of shore birds and migrating ducks. There are marshes, mud flats and open water to enjoy. The marsh is a beautiful place to walk – the trail is right on the water, with the Bay Area's picturesque skylines and hills as a backdrop.

The hike is easy and flat, along a wide (wheelchair-accessible) trail on top of dikes and boardwalks. Park activities include walking and biking. There is great picnicking on benches along the trail. The interpretive center is staffed by naturalists. No dogs or horses are allowed. No fee.

To reach the trailhead from the intersection of Interstates 580 and 238 in San Leandro, take I-238 west 2 miles to I-880. Head south on I-880 4 miles to CA Hwy. 92. Take Hwy. 92 west 1.8 miles to Clawiter Road. From the offramp, head straight across Clawiter to Breakwater Road. Follow Breakwater Road 1 mile to the Hayward Shoreline Interpretive Center. Park beside the road in front of the interpretive center.

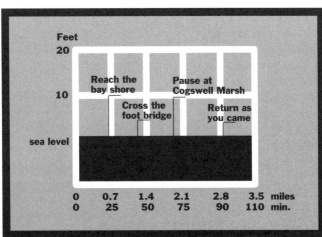

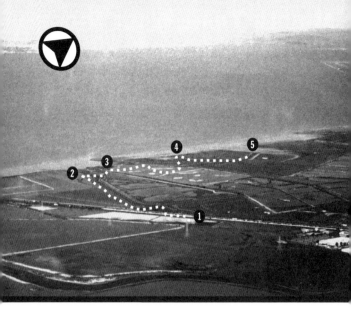

Step By Step

1 The Marsh Trail begins at the dirt road several yards east of the interpretive center. Pass through the metal gate and walk west, passing the Hayward Regional Shoreline signs near the interpretive center (5 min.).

2 Continue along the Marsh Trail as it passes through a freshwater marsh full of shore birds – willets, terns, cormorants, egrets, sandpipers, pelicans and migrating ducks – toward the open waters of San Francisco Bay. As the Marsh Trail reaches the bay shore, it turns north, following the shoreline (25 min.).

3 Follow the Marsh Trail as it winds along the shoreline of the bay to the intersection of a trail that branches off to the right. Stay on the path to the left (40 min.).

4 Continue along the shoreline to a foot bridge (45 min.).

5 Cross the foot bridge and walk along the shoreline levee to a bench. At this point, the levee turns east to enter Cogswell Marsh (55 min.).

● Enjoy the views from this bench, which lies outside the restored Cogswell Marsh. After bird watching and contemplation, retrace your steps to the parking area (1 hour, 50 min.).

"The marsh is a beautiful place to walk – right on the water, with the Bay Area's picturesque skylines and hills as a backdrop."

BRIDLE TRAIL/WEST RIDGE TRAIL/ORCHARD TRAIL LOOP

Redwood Regional Park

Trail Length:
1.7 miles

Drive Time From
I-580 in Oakland:
15 minutes

Approx. Time:
1 hour 10 min.

Elevation change:
500 feet

5

Redwood Regional Park lies in the wooded hills behind the city of Oakland. The land is shrouded in a blanket of the historic coastal redwood forest that once covered the region. Some of the trees tower to 100 feet, but it wasn't always so. Back in the logging days of the 1800s, this region buzzed with sawmills and shantytowns.

The hike is relatively strenuous, along sometimes steep trails. The route is wide, and easily shared with bikes and horses. The trails lead up from Redwood Creek to the ridge, then back down through a redwood forest. Park activities include horseback riding, biking, hiking and picnicking. No horses or bikes are allowed on the Orchard Trail. Dogs must be on leash. No fee.

To reach the trailhead from the intersection of Interstate 580 and California Highway 13 in Oakland, take Hwy. 13 north 1.5 miles to Redwood Road. Take Redwood Road east 4.5 miles to Redwood Regional Park. Park in the lot on the left, by Fishway Site.

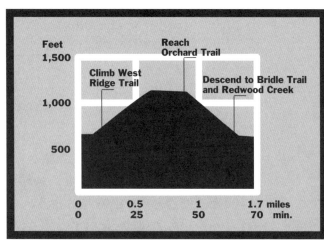

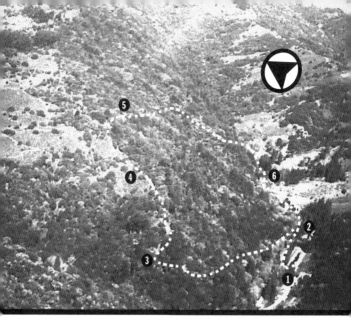

Step By Step

❶ Walk to the west end of the parking area, past the interpretive sign near the fishway, and cross the bridge. Walk right (east) along the Bridle Trail to intersection of West Ridge Trail (5 min.).

❷ Walk left (west), following West Ridge Trail up through the forest. The road turns to the north, exposing a view of a wooded valley below, before reaching the intersection of a side trail leading to Golden Spike Trail. Follow West Ridge Trail as it turns to the right (20 min.).

❸ Climb steeply through a eucalyptus forest. Ascend several switchbacks and steep sections of trail before you reach the intersection of Toyon Trail (35 min.).

❹ Follow the West Ridge Trail straight ahead (northwest) along the top of the ridge to its intersection with the French Trail and the Orchard Trail (45 min.).

❺ Turn right on the Orchard Trail and walk down steep switchbacks through oak, maple, madrone, bay and redwood trees to the Bridle Trail, which meanders along Redwood Creek (1 hour).

❻ Walk right on the Bridle Trail and head back to the parking area (1 hour, 10 min.).

"This land is shrouded in a blanket of the historic coastal redwood forest that once covered the region."

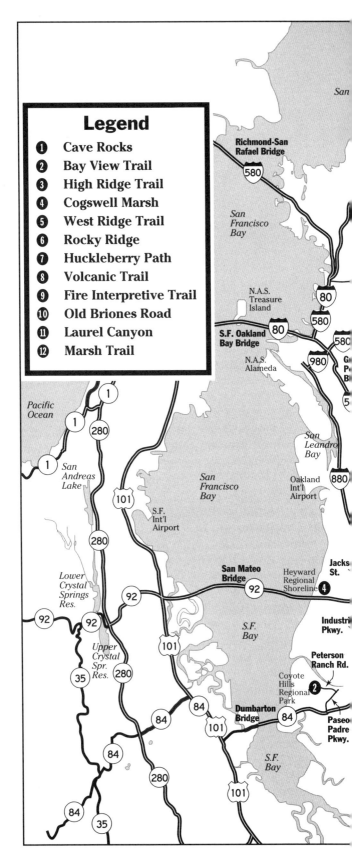

Legend

1. Cave Rocks
2. Bay View Trail
3. High Ridge Trail
4. Cogswell Marsh
5. West Ridge Trail
6. Rocky Ridge
7. Huckleberry Path
8. Volcanic Trail
9. Fire Interpretive Trail
10. Old Briones Road
11. Laurel Canyon
12. Marsh Trail

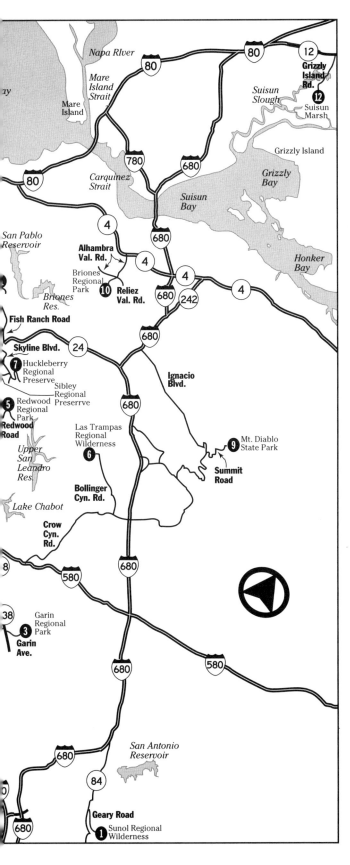

ROCKY RIDGE TRAIL TO ROCK 2

Las Trampas Regional Wilderness

Trail Length:
2.6 miles

Drive Time From
I-580 in Dublin:
15 minutes

Approx. Time:
2 hours

Elevation change:
800 feet

6

Las Trampas is Spanish for "The Traps," which were set in the chaparral to capture elk that roamed these hills in the previous century. The Rocky Ridge side of Las Trampas Regional Wilderness is rolling grassland spotted with oak and bay forests. Rocky Ridge rises to just more than 2,000 feet, with intriguing rock formations that have been sculpted by wind and painted with lichen.

The hike is an easy, gentle climb along a wide, paved trail. There are great views from the ridge top. Park activities include horseback riding, walking, wildlife viewing and picnicking. Dogs must be on leash. No bikes are allowed. No fee.

To reach the trailhead from the intersection of Interstates 580 and 680 in Dublin, take I-680 north 4.8 miles to Bollinger Canyon Road. Turn right onto Bollinger Canyon Road and continue north for 5.3 miles to the entry gate to Las Trampas Regional Wilderness. Continue until the road ends. Turn left into the parking/picnic area. The trailhead is across the driveway to the northwest.

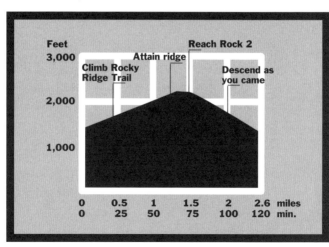

Step By Step

❶ Begin in the northwest end of the parking area. Walk west along the paved Rocky Ridge Trail, passing through a metal gate. The trail wanders through open grassland, making occasional dips into small forests of oak and bay trees. Follow the path as it climbs to 1,600 feet and the intersection of Cuesta Trail (45 min.).

❷ Stay to the right, continuing along Rocky Ridge Trail. The route climbs gradually toward the top of the ridge. The trail swings back around to the south to the intersection of the Upper Trail and the Rocky Ridge Loop Trail (55 min.).

❸ Walk to the right, staying on the paved Rocky Ridge Trail. The trail eventually turns south to the second intersection of the Rocky Ridge Loop Trail, which leads to Rock 2 (1 hour).

❹ Leaving the paved trail, walk left (southwest) along Rocky Ridge Loop Trail to the summit region of Rock 2 (1 hour, 15 min.). From here, several trails explore the ridge region. Use one of these trails if you'd like to take a longer hike.

❺ Finish the loop onto the paved trail and retrace your steps to the parking area (2 hours).

"Rocky Ridge rises to just more than 2,000 feet, with intriguing rock formations that have been sculpted by the wind and painted with lichen."

HUCKLEBERRY PATH

Huckleberry Botanic Regional Preserve

 Trail Length:
1.7 miles

 Drive Time From
I-580 in Oakland:
20 minutes

 Approx. Time:
1 hr. 45 min.

Elevation change:
200 feet

7

There are plants in the Huckleberry Botanic Regional Preserve that exist nowhere else in the East Bay. Instead of the expected oak woodland, coastal chamise and manzanita cover the hills. These plants normally live only in select coastal areas where the climate and soils are just right, such as off the coast of central California. It's assumed that Huckleberry's plant species originated long ago, when the bay's climate was warmer.

The hike is tricky, along sometimes steep and narrow trails. The route leads into a wooded canyon, then to the top of a ridge. Park activities include walking, picnicking and nature study. No dogs, horses or bikes are allowed on the Huckleberry Path. No fee.

To reach the trailhead from the intersection of Interstate 580 and California Highway 24 in Oakland, take Hwy. 24 east 8 miles to Fish Ranch Road. Go right on Fish Ranch 0.8 miles to Grizzly Peak Boulevard. Take Grizzly Peak left 2.4 miles to Skyline Boulevard. Turn left on Skyline and go 2 miles to the Huckleberry Botanic Regional Preserve parking lot.

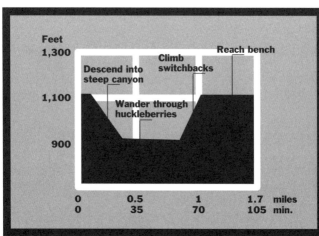

Step By Step

1 Walk right (southeast), through the gate, on the Huckleberry Path. Hike through the picnic area and past preserve signs to the intersection of Huckleberry Loop (5 min.).

2 Walk left (northeast), down through an oak and bay forest and into a steep canyon. Reach an opening in the fence at the intersection of East Bay Ridge Trail (20 min.).

3 Walk up to the right (southeast) along Huckleberry Path under a canopy of bay trees amid the ferns and huckleberries that adorn the trail. Cross a drainage (30 min.).

4 The trail passes into and out of ravines before intersecting the East Bay Skyline Ridge Trail and Huckleberry Self-Guiding Nature Path (1 hour).

5 Walk up to the right (southwest), ascending switchbacks, then steps to the ridge. Reach another intersection with Huckleberry Self-Guiding Nature Path (1 hour, 10 min.).

6 Walk left. The path traverses the west side of the canyon, then descends stairs back into the bay forest (1 hour, 30 min.).

7 Continue northwest through a forest to a bench overlooking Mount Diablo and nearby Sibley Volcanic Preserve (1 hour, 35 min.)

8 Continue northwest along Huckleberry Path to intersect the Huckleberry Loop Trail (1 hour, 40 min.).

9 Continue straight (left) to the parking area (1 hour, 45 min.).

"It's assumed Huckleberry's plant species originated long ago..."

ROUND TOP LOOP TRAIL/ VOLCANIC TRAIL

Sibley Volcanic Regional Preserve

 Trail Length:
2 miles

 Drive Time From I-580 in Oakland:
15 minutes

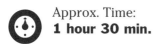 Approx. Time:
1 hour 30 min.

 Elevation change:
250 feet

8

This nook in the Berkeley and Oakland hills is alive with geologic hints of the operation of an ancient volcano. Apparently, 9.5 million years ago, Round Top was the center of a great volcanic cauldron. The outside of the volcano eroded, leaving the center exposed. Faults folded the volcano on its side, exposing the entire vent system. The main vent of the ancient volcano, as well as basaltic dikes, lava flows and red-baked cinder piles, can be seen along the Volcanic Trail.

The hike is easy, along wide trails that climb gently. The route explores some volcanic deposits, then circles the core of the volcano and descends into the woods. Park activities include walking, horseback riding and biking. No fee.

To reach the trailhead from the intersection of Interstate 580 and California Highway 24 in Oakland, take Hwy. 24 east 8 miles to Fish Ranch Road. Go 0.8 miles west on Fish Ranch Road to Grizzly Peak Boulevard. Turn left (south) on Grizzly Peak and go 2.4 miles to Skyline Boulevard. Turn left on Skyline and go 100 yards to the preserve entrance on the left.

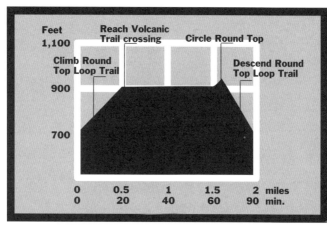

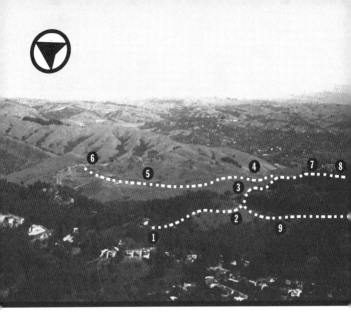

Step By Step

1 Walk to the right (east) side of the visitor center and through the brown gate. Follow the paved Round Top Loop Trail through the woods. Reach a "Y" intersection (5 min.).

2 Veer right onto Round Top Loop Trail/Volcanic Trail, and go through a cattle gate (10 min.).

3 Continue north along Round Top Loop Trail/Volcanic Trail to where the trails diverge (20 min.).

4 Walk left on Volcanic Trail to an intersection where the Volcanic Trail veers right (25 min.).

5 Stay right (northwest), following Volcanic Trail up the hill to a signpost marking Volcanic Trail. Go left (northwest) to basaltic lava flows and signpost #9 (40 min.).

6 Retrace your steps to the intersection of Volcanic Trail and Round Top Loop Trail (1 hour).

7 Continue on Round Top Loop Trail past a quarry at signpost #4 to an intersection where Round Top Loop Trail veers to the right (south) (1 hour, 5 min.).

8 Go right on Round Top Loop Trail (now a foot path) and climb around Round Top. Pass a cattle gate and circle the volcano. Reach the intersection of Bay Ridge Trail (1 hour, 15 min.).

9 Veer right (northwest), staying on Round Top Loop Trail to its intersection with the paved road. Turn left on the road, heading downhill (west). Walk past the "Y" intersection to the parking area (1 hour, 30 min.).

"...Round Top was the center of a great volcanic cauldron."

FIRE INTERPRETIVE TRAIL

Mount Diablo State Park

Trail Length:
0.7 mile

Drive Time From
I-580 in Oakland:
50 minutes

Approx. Time:
40 minutes

Elevation change:
minimal

9

At **3,849 feet, Mount Diablo** provides the highest vantage point in the Bay Area. On a clear day from the observation deck, you can see Mount Lassen, 181 miles to the north. This loop circles just below the top of the mountain, offering 360-degree views of the seemingly boundless open space of the East Bay hills below.

The walk is easy and flat along a partially paved (wheelchair-accessible) trail. Park activities include picnicking, walking and camping in designated areas. No dogs are allowed. There is a small fee.

To reach the trailhead from the intersection of Interstate 580 and California Highway 24 in Oakland, take Hwy. 24 east 15 miles to Interstate 680. Take I-680 north 1 mile to Ygnacio Valley Drive. Turn right and go east 2.6 miles on Ygnacio Valley, to a right on Walnut Avenue. Drive south on Walnut Avenue for 1.6 miles to Oak Grove. Turn right on Oak Grove and head south 50 feet to North Gate Road. Turn left on North Gate Road to the park entrance. Follow North Gate Road 8.5 miles to Summit Road. Turn left on Summit Road and drive 4.2 miles to the Lower Summit parking lot.

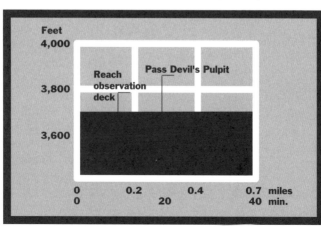

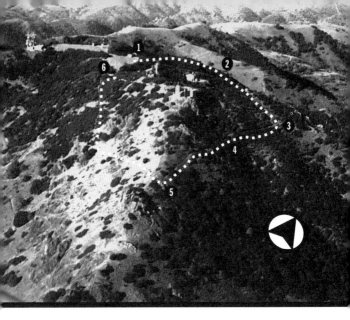

Step By Step

1 The trail leaves from the north side of Summit Road at the point where it splits into two one-way streets above the lower parking lot. Walk north across Summit Road to the start of the Fire Interpretive Trail.

2 Walk east along the paved trail, through an oak grove, to the observation deck and enjoy the spectacular views (10 min.).

3 From the deck, the paved trail turns to the south, and becomes a dirt foot path. Circle the east flank of Mount Diablo, with a view of North Peak in the foreground (15 min.).

4 Continue along the foot path through the chaparral. A fire, which chaparral thrives on, burned much of this area in 1977. Continue to the rock outcrop at Devil's Pulpit (20 min.).

5 From Devil's Pulpit, the trail turns west and traverses through oak and grassland on the south face of Mount Diablo (30 min.).

6 Continue around the mountain, passing through a mini-forest of juniper, yerba santa and chamise, until you rejoin the Summit Road at the parking area where you started (40 min.).

"This loop circles just below the top of the mountain, offering 360-degree views of the seemingly boundless open space of the East Bay hills below."

OLD BRIONES ROAD TO MOTT PEAK RIDGE

Briones Regional Park

Trail Length:
2.4 miles

Drive Time From I-580 in Berkeley:
30 minutes

Approx. Time:
1 hour 30 min.

Elevation change:
200 feet

10 **Briones Regional Park rests** in the ranch and farm land of the Alhambra Valley. The Old Briones Road meanders through pastoral grassland to a ridge offering abundant views. There are several lagoons along the road – naturally occurring vernal pools that served as watering holes in the cattle ranching days. From a bench on Mott Peak Ridge, you can watch the sunset and see the lay of the land from the Suisun Marsh and the Carquinez Straight to the Central Valley beyond.

The hike is easy, along wide trails that climb gently. Park activities include hiking, horseback riding, biking and picnicking. Dogs must be on leash. No fee.

To reach the trailhead from the intersection of Interstates 580 and 80 in Berkeley, take I-80 east 10 miles to California Highway 4 in Pinole. Take Hwy. 4 east 10 miles to Alhambra Avenue in Martinez. Turn right on Alhambra and go south 0.6 mile to Alhambra Valley Road. Go right 1.6 miles on Alhambra Valley to Briones Road. Turn left on Briones Road and go 1.5 miles to the gate at the trailhead. Park along the side of the road.

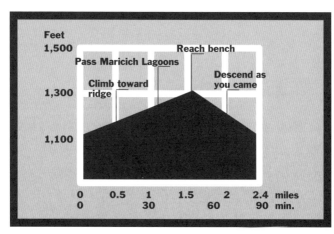

Feet
1,500

Pass Maricich Lagoons

Reach bench

Climb toward ridge

Descend as you came

1,300

1,100

| 0 | 0.5 | 1 | 1.5 | 2 | 2.4 | miles |
| 0 | | 30 | | 60 | 90 | min. |

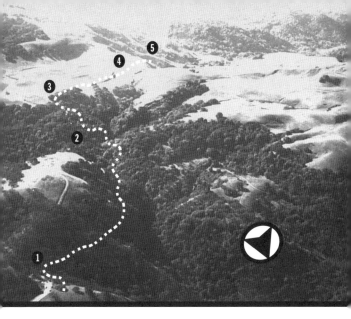

Step By Step

① The trailhead is at the gate at the south end of the road. Walk through the gate, passing the park sign. Follow Old Briones Road as it gradually climbs through a forest of bay, oak and madrone to a gate at the top of a knoll. This is also the intersection of an un-marked road off to the right (30 min.).

② Stay to the left (east), following the Old Briones Road to its intersection with Spengler Trail at Maricich Lagoons (35 min.).

③ Turn right, staying on Old Briones Road as it climbs through open grassland to the ridge that rises to the west.

Reach the first inter-section of Old Briones Road and Briones Crest Trail (45 min.).

④ Continue straight/left on Old Briones Road to its next intersection with the Briones Crest Trail (50 min.).

⑤ Turn right (southwest) along Old Briones Road, then immediately turn right (northwest) again. You will walk around the back side of the fence that runs along the side of Old Briones Road. Follow the foot path that leads to a bench atop Mott Peak ridge, and enjoy the sights (55 min).

● Retrace your steps to the parking area (1 hour, 30 min.).

"Old Briones Road meanders through pastoral grassland to a ridge offering abundant views."

LAUREL CANYON LOOP

Tilden Regional Park

Trail Length:
2.5 miles

Drive Time From
I-580 in Berkeley:
20 minutes

Approx. Time:
1 hour 45 min.

Elevation change:
300 feet

11

Tilden Regional Park lies in a quiet valley just east of Berkeley. Tilden Nature Area, home of the Laurel Canyon Loop, is in the quieter north end of the park.

The walk is strenuous, with a continuous climb up Laurel Canyon. Park activities include hiking, biking, horseback riding, picnicking and camping by permit. No bikes are allowed on Laurel Canyon Trail. No dogs are permitted. No fee. The trails are marked with logos; the Laurel Canyon Trail logo is a bay single leaf with a single bay berry.

To reach the trailhead from Interstate 580 in Berkeley, take the University Avenue exit. Follow University east 2.1 miles to Oxford Street. Turn left on Oxford St. and go north 0.5 miles to Rose Street. Turn right on Rose St. for 0.1 miles to Spruce Street. Follow Spruce Street for 0.8 mile northeast, across Grizzly Peak Boulevard, to Canon Drive. Turn left on Canon Drive and go to Central Park Avenue. Turn left from Central Park Ave. into the Tilden parking area.

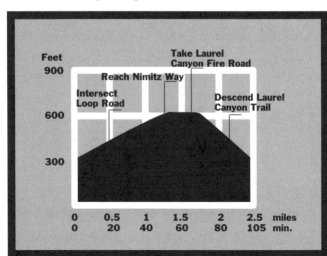

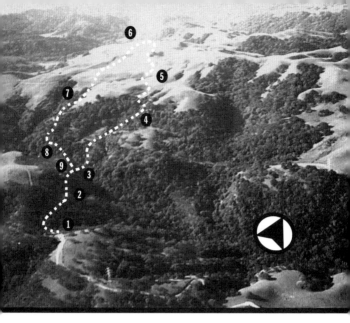

Step By Step

1 Walk northeast from the education center. Go straight uphill along the fence, just left of Little Farm. At the top of the hill, walk left (northwest) on the dirt road 100 feet to Laurel Canyon Trail on the right (10 min.).

2 Take Laurel Canyon through a eucalyptus grove to Loop Road. Walk left (north) along Loop Road 100 feet to the intersection of Laurel Canyon Trail to the right (20 min.).

3 Walk right (north) along Laurel Canyon. Pass the intersection of Pine Tree Trail (30 min.).

4 Go left (northeast) up the canyon to a trail fork marked by a sign to "Nimitz Way" (50 min.).

5 Continue right. The trail crosses the canyon and spills into a meadow. Go north to the unmarked Laurel Canyon Fire Road intersection (1 hour).

6 Walk left (west) on Laurel Canyon Fire Road, down the hill past Pear Trail (1 hour, 10 min.).

7 Continue down (west) on the fire road to the intersection of Loop Road (1 hour, 25 min.).

8 Walk left (south) on Loop Road to its intersection with Laurel Canyon Trail (1 hr. 30 min.).

9 Walk right (southwest) on Laurel Canyon (now a foot path) to the intersection of a dirt road to the left, which is marked by a sign. The road leads to the visitor center (1 hour, 35 min.).

● Walk left on the dirt road to the parking area (1 hour, 45 min.).

MARSH TRAIL

Rush Ranch, Suisun Marsh

Trail Length:
2.2 miles

Drive Time From
I-580 in Berkeley:
45 minutes

Approx. Time:
1 hour 40 min.

Elevation change:
50 feet

12

Rush Ranch offers some of the most inviting hiking in all of the Suisun Marsh, the largest estuarine marsh in the United States.

The ranch is at the west end of the marsh, set against the Potrero Hills. You'll hike among cattails and tules, river otters, tule elk, ducks, ring-tailed pheasants, northern harriers, short-eared owls and golden eagles. In all, there are more than 230 species of birds known to pass through the marsh.

The hike is easy, along flat dikes and trails. The route heads out over open marshland, loops around to the main slough, then returns through a field to the ranch. Park activities include hiking, picnicking and bird-watching. There is a visitor center at the ranch. No pets are allowed. No smoking is permitted. No fee.

To reach the trailhead from the intersection of Interstates 580 and 80 in Berkeley, take I-80 east 35 to CA Hwy. 12. Take Hwy. 12 east 4 miles to Grizzly Island Road in Fairfield. Turn right on Grizzly Island and go 2.2 miles to Rush Ranch on the right. Park in the lot.

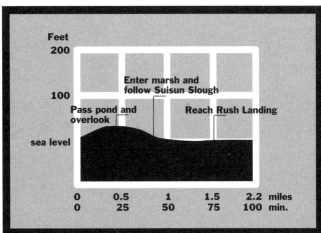

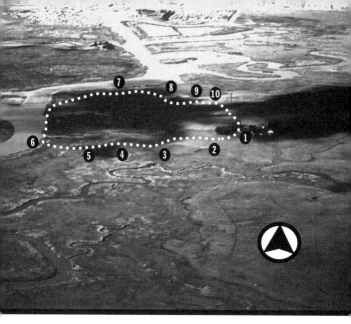

Step By Step

1 From the parking area, walk south past the ranch buildings. The visitor center is on the right (west).

2 The Marsh Trail leaves from the rear (west) deck of the visitor center. Walk west through eucalyptus into a meadow (5 min.).

3 Pass a pond on the right just before you reach a gate. A sign with an arrow directs you left (south). In a few feet, an overlook sign (also with an arrow) directs you right (west), over the hill to a bench overlooking the marsh (20 min.).

4 Continuing west, the trail descends back into the marsh to the intersection with a trail that circles the bottom of a hill (25 min.).

5 Turn right (north) and follow Marsh Trail toward an old gate. Turn left (west) as the trail curves through the marsh (30 min.).

6 Pass a flood gate as the trail curves right (north) to follow Suisun Slough (40 min.).

7 Pass along the shore of the main slough to a gate (1 hour, 10 min.).

8 Reach the bench near Rush Landing, which overlooks the slough and Fairfield's harbor (1 hour, 15 min.).

9 The trail winds right (south), toward an alkaline pond (1 hour, 20 min.).

10 Walk over dirt piled at the south end of the pond. Cross the plank and pass the gate. The trail veers right (southeast), back to the ranch (1 hour, 40 min.).

"You'll hike among cattails and tules...owls and golden eagles."

BOOKS IN THE
12 SHORT HIKES SERIES

COLORADO

DENVER AREA:
12 Short Hikes: Boulder
12 Short Hikes: Denver Foothills North
12 Short Hikes: Denver Foothills Central
12 Short Hikes: Denver Foothills South

COLORADO MOUNTAINS:
12 Short Hikes: Aspen
12 Short Hikes: Steamboat Springs
12 Short Hikes: Summit County
12 Short Hikes: Vail

ROCKY MOUNTAIN NATIONAL PARK:
12 Short Hikes: East Side
12 Short Hikes: West Side

CALIFORNIA

SAN FRANCISCO AREA:
12 Short Hikes: North Bay
12 Short Hikes: South Bay
12 Short Hikes: East Bay
12 Short Hikes: Coast

SAN DIEGO AREA:
12 Short Hikes: Mountains
12 Short Hikes: Coast

CALIFORNIA MOUNTAINS:
12 Short Hikes: Mammoth Lakes

WASHINGTON STATE

MOUNT RAINIER NATIONAL PARK:
12 Short Hikes: Sunrise
12 Short Hikes: Paradise

Address all comments, additions or corrections to the author, in care of Chockstone Press, P.O. Box 3505, Evergreen, Colorado 80437. Orders for this or other books in this series may be made by writing to the above address or by calling Chockstone Press at (303) 674-6888 or (800)337-5012.